The Road to Infinity

A Man's Journey Towards Himself

The Road to Infinity

A Man's Journey Towards Himself

Dr. Tanbir Dhingra

Ocean Paperbacks
A Division of Ocean Books Pvt. Ltd.
ISO 9001:2008 Publishers

Published by
Ocean Paperbacks
A Division of Ocean Books Pvt. Ltd.
4/19 Asaf Ali Road,
New Delhi-110 002 (INDIA)
e-mail: info@oceanbooks.in

ISBN 978-81-8430-507-4
THE ROAD TO INFINITY
by Dr. Tanbir Dhingra

Edition
First, 2017

Price
₹ 200.00 (Rupees Two Hundred only)

Printed at
R-Tech Offset Printers, Delhi

DEDICATION

To ***Every Person*** I've met in my life, who inspired it and will not read it.

To all the ***Amazing Women*** I've met, thanks for giving such courage to me to pen down all my emotions on paper.

To ***Everyone*** who wonders if I am writing about them in these pages. I am.

Author's Note

I remember receiving a phone call from *Apoorva* saying that my writings have moved the founder, *Ocean Books Pvt. Ltd.* in quite a way that he said, he had admired such literary work before also but mine was way too deeply thoughtful to take in, contrary to my young age. I took a long sigh; looked in the mirror and thought to myself, "So, my first book is going to be published!" I was struggling to establish myself as a writer and to follow my path; despite all the voices were telling me it was impossible.

"Every second is a moment and every moment is a thought, in the mind—the master weaver of words. Either it's expressing my heart's elation or just lament about my failures; everything which demands to be felt is worthy of words as they may have hitherto woven in ignorance and pain, they may now weave in enlightenment and happiness."

The following poem is taken from a collection of *reflections* and *narrative poems* written by Me.

The Theory of LIFE ... ***'THE BROKEN LOVE'***

Walking on the road leading to your destiny,
You Meet Someone

Someone to fall in love with, someone to be with you chose
That night in hands with a red rose and in that romantic way you propose
You Two Get Close

The taken away of your breath, on your face that unreasonable smile
It's All Great For A While

That long 'Break-up & Patch-up' stories
Those sleepless nights with endless crying
Then One Stops Trying

Those ego problems, those misunderstanding ones situations
Changing into life drowning and love killing frustrations
You talk less.
All Those Love Expressions Turns To Awkward Conversations

Repent, regret and that rifting
Finally there's strangling of your expectations,
The Drifting

The promises which were meant to keep forever
No longer seems to be fulfilled never
No Communications Whatsoever

The love is buried alive in that deadly cascade
Forgetting the meaning; for each other they were made
Memories Start To Fade

Then that person you know
Becomes A Person You Once Knew

That's how it usually goes, right?
Sad Isn't It … </3

—Dr. Tanbir Dhingra

Acknowledgement

First and foremost, a special feeling of gratitude to *My God* '**MOM & DAD**', *Parminder* and *Narinder Dhingra*, it's impossible to thank you enough for everything you've done; raising me such a good human being, always being there and believing in me and also providing me with every comfort every facility you could by working so hard each day and night, 365 days a year without a single holiday.

To my **Elder Sister** *Dr. Jasneet*, M.S., thanks for the wonderful memories of growing up since day one, and holding your finger has helped me to accomplish so many achievements in life since school, medical college and way more ahead. I still remember the ending line to your essays, *"All we need is imagination and determination.* "This has changed my perspective towards life.

To my **companion** *Apoorva Bhargava*, who is my daily reminder of all that is good in this world. You give me hope, positivity and strength.

To my childhood **best friend** *Amrinder Singh*, always being there by my side guiding me even though he was wrong not always but yeah sometimes. I love you brother.

RELATIONSHIP

"I stepped into this
Relationship
not to step out again."

THE VOW

*"I promise to be **Patient**,*
Coz I believe in you,
The person you will
grow out to be
And the couple we will
be together

*I promise to be **Kind**,*
Coz, now I will bend
down on my knees
(ring in hands)
And with open hands
will pray
To figure out the
problems for you ever
No matter how I suffer
for you in which way

I promise to help you

Love Life,

From holding your

hands in joy

To holding you tight in

sorrows

Withstanding the

failures through

To admiring our success

together

Coz, I promise to be

there for you

Now and forever

I promise to ***Love YOU,***
And to be there,
whenever and wherever
you need me
Coz when two people are
meant for each other
No distance is too far
No time is too long; I'll
be there (a long sigh)

Until today and till the
day of my grief

Never, ever want to leave
you or
live without you
I will walk with you
hand in hand
Wherever our journey
leads us
Living, Learning, and
***Loving** together*
Coz, I promise to be
there for you
Now and forever

I told you before and I'm
telling you now
I know no other than
this way
Coz I'm falling for you.
Falling for you with
each day."

*"A Life without Love
will have no Roses
But a Life with Love
will have some Thorns."*

"I worship you like
my Real Heaven
and Stairway to You is
my Pure, Soulful
Eternal Love."

"Just not so far I walked with you to only be a friend.

Every moment is a new beginning, every failure is a new start

Coz for me it never was, never is and never gona be 'The End'."

"Occupancy doesn't mean there ain't a vacancy in my heart
Bribe me with love
Either it could be remorse or forever
I'll be yours."

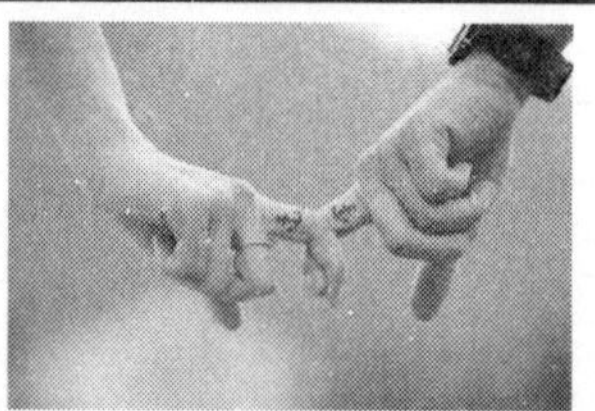

"LOVE in real is only understood when you overcome the feel of 'Infatuation' and feel the pain of letting go off someone knowing it inside that they can't be replaced by anyone else, never, no matter how much beautifully great the other person is."

"True Love Got Once Must Be Fought For

A moment of negligence may break the very heart which loved you against all the odds.

Coz Real Love isn't leaving him for just one thing he did wrong to you but loving him for all the things he did right to you always."

"ARE YOU GIVING TIME TO YOUR LOVED ONES?

You might be busy with your work but your shouldn't be busy for the people you love! The work left uncompleted can be counted as pending but once that person left you would leave behind a regret pending which can never be completed again."

"My love, you are a piece of my body and mine eternal soul. Without you puzzle of my life is incomplete like I'm incomplete without you." Without you, I'm nothing but someone standing alone with a feeling of love still to be adored or admired.

You deserve to be loved more than I love my life coz you mean the whole world to me. Loving you is what you deserve and getting back the essence of love makes me believe that I'm worth to deserve for what I am and when I'm with you. Your love wants me to be like the way you are to me."

"Everything with you is better than anything without you, I'm better with you."

Are you lucky in Love? "Not everyone is lucky to feel love. Love is a definition still to be defined. It can't be found at some place, it can't be borrowed, it can't be bought with money. You can only feel the feel of love if you're pure from inside like your love is.

Love you see around is a fragrance of the words, feelings and emotions you express and what in actual makes you as a whole. Love seek no ages, no fortunes but moments of impacts. Nor the people do last neither do their words but the soulful moments with soulful hearts. Know this thing, you are lucky if you ever had been in love."

"Destiny is a pull created by two dumb people, No matter how hard they try to do the 'Right in Right' like the others do but they'll always do the 'Right in Left' because it's

not them but their own 'FATE' which dragged them to meet and made it happened in a way which with some other dumb, it wouldn't be that way for them. It's how the destiny works but not everyone does follow it and see how life could be more beautiful than being the way it turned out to be."

"LOVE: That is inexplicable, which itself is a definition still to be defined... can't be expressed but can be felt in different stages or moments of life. Love doesn't require words but actions to show the real meaning of being fallen for someone in actual."

"Favours do make relationships Dishonouring and ignoring doesn't."

"The love story of two strangers is the best story till that strangeness between them is not over."

"I might not be knowing as many 'hashtags' to tag just one picture of us my friend but a tag of lifeline to our role-plays in 'The Story of My Life', so far i.e. 'BROTHER'."

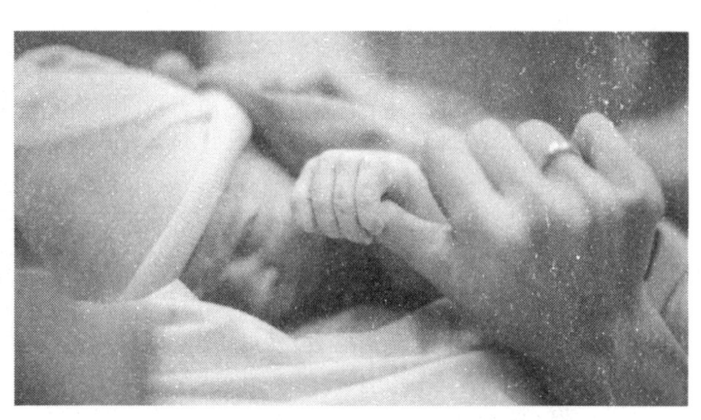

"With my SAFE HAVEN secluding all the Negatives and perceiving all the Positives and that's you Mother."

"If love was to look at you and feel every second of it, I can do it everyday."

"You can't even implicate when the odds does complicate."

"Don't bound yourself until things doesn't make up right."

"These late night talks, these limitless chit chats, and this overwhelming care for you, all are not just a matter of being getting 'Friend Zoned' one day until either my mind or my heart realises a mistake of judging my own feelings and my

own fate to be wrong every time. Coz I believe in true love and it can't be a lie, and if it is so then these Destiny and God, both are two big lies created by Humans and I shall leave my body behind with these soulless human bodies and let my soul begin an quest to search the meaning of life."

"I shared this memory because this was the day I could feel myself I could breathe despite of false air exhaled by others. No superiority

No inferiority imposed
because this is our
romance which requires
no money to be counted
coz we think its endless
and sharing happiness
instead of sorrows coz not
doing this is useless."

"To die and part, is less difficult I ever find. But to part and die, it will tear me from inside."

In life at some point somewhere someone needs someone in some corner of life for sometime to sum up all the positives and subtracting all the negatives.

EMOTIONS

"Sometimes I want to scream my pain at the top of my lungs. But then I see this selfish world is deaf."

"The only reason you won't let go off what is making you sad is because it was the only thing that made you happy. With a beautiful person comes the beautiful memories which can't be lived again with someone else the way you did with the one you felt complete with."

"Sometimes You Can't Just Let Go Off What Is Not Yours, But Sometimes You Just Let Go Off To See If Ever It Was Yours."

Strange but true!

"I will always stand by your side
...But never for someone put me behind
...I trust you blindly so much
...But never prove me a blind."

"Pearls are a special gift which I'll gather one by one to make a beautiful necklace for you,

...Same like pearls are the moments which are a special gift I'll gather one by one to make a beautiful life for you."

"GOOD-BYE isn't that painful until you satisfy yourself with an explanation, ...which in actual was never explained."

"These tears that I cry may not mean nothing to anyone anymore...
But I still manage to overcome all those sad sorrows that lay beneath my skin."

"Meaning of true love
fades away
When you are no longer
obsessed
With the feeling to
possess it."

A SWEET CONVERSATION BETWEEN ME AND MY LOVE.

She said, ARE YOU SCARED OF DEATH?

I said, "I'm not scared to being dead,

I'm scared of not being with you."

"Probability of falling for me starts with a countdown the moment you see me and if there's still a miss meeting me in person can rest assure."

"Talking is revealing yourself to the people, so talk. And judging is revealing of themselves to you, so stop!"

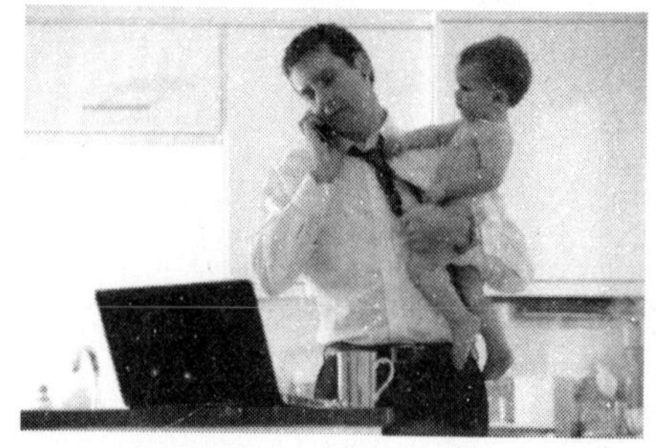

"Today's generation might not consider but every father's story is a self-made man story. You don't need biopics or biographies to be one but being extraordinarily hardworker to chase your dreams like your father did once."

"My scars could heal, especially the ones on the outside."

"For Dad

A man who taught me
to be a man from a boy.
A man who used to hold
me and make me stand
on my feet on his hand to
make me see how higher

I can achieve in life when he's with me. A man who sacrificed his life to make my life. A man so simple but charming enough to give me such genes that I'm really thankful for."

"You know what's the best part about doing for someone is? You just do it no matter what and why, even if you don't want to but you do it knowing

that the consequences could be potentially harmful but you do it coz you wana do it for them. And that's what Serendipitous Love is."

"So is it still cold or you need a blanket made of 'me' stuff to keep you cozy throughout."

"I gave you everything but you gave me none. How mesmerising it used to be. When two was better than one."

"How can I disconnect from someone with whom I really want to connect."

TIME

Is your Life made up of just Time only or by Moments?

"Life isn't made up of time with standardised values to be counted, but of moments to be lived. Moments that we make

when we are around the ones we love. Each second is a moment to be made so special which we can't let go off simply coz time once gone will just leave two things behind. One, the regrets and second, the memories just not spent but lived with the person when we were at the age to love, fall and get broken. Neither will this time come back nor the age to feel the way we feel for everything now." So, live life before it's gone!

"You'll fight with your Best Friend. You'll blame a New Love for things an Old one did.

You'll Cry because Time is passing too Fast and you'll eventually Lose Someone you Love.

So, take too many Pictures, Laugh too much, and Love like you've never been Hurt because 'Every Sixty Seconds You Spend Upset Is A Minute Of Happiness You'll Never Get Back'."

TODAY is a Gift, that's why it is being called SURPRISE."

"Live your life, Take chances, Be crazy!! Don't wait because right now is the oldest you've ever been and youngest you'll be ever again.

—What if, you wake

up next morning; you wanted to live your life but all you realise is that you've got less time to live but survive.

—What if, that once chance taking could've brought you the best thing that could've had ever happened to you in your life but you didn't.

—What if, you regret your life coz all you did

was lived in pride or hadn't any time to let go off and explore yourself to find who you are and how much craziest you could ever be.

—Life is too short, why to be afraid of living it to your fullest. So, go out and fall in love coz all you have to experience those 'Once in a Lifetime Experiences'."

"LIFE is
'Perfectly Perfect'
with the perfect change
in time with the perfect
change in you."

"Friendship isn't about how long we take it but it's about how strong we make it."

Coz that one precious friend could cost you your hundred

or thousand joyous moments. Likewise, the moments are the ones we want to hold on tight after they're gone. May be we'll meet thousands of persons ahead in our life but those thousands can never fill the empty space of that one precious person gone forever."

"Life seems to be short, when you want to LIVE it. ...But Life seems to be too long, when you want to SURVIVE it."

"Time runs always at the same speed for everyone. But it's only you who lives within the change of the time or changes the time for better living."

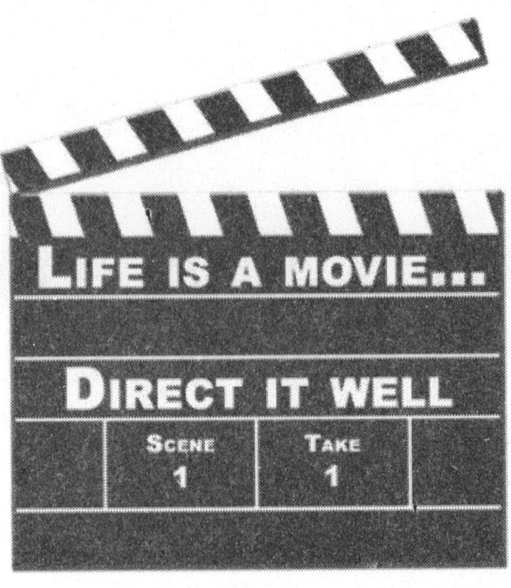

"Live each act in your life to it's fullest coz you never know.... Till when your 'Roleplay' in this story last."

"Never make it too late

coz

EITHER you'll lose the person who loved you from yesterday...

OR you'll lose the person until you realize to love them till tomorrow."

"Time flees away fast but Memories never do, they stay within us, no matter how long you live at one time you'll flashback them all."

"A wait till Infinity and our immortal souls destined for Eternity."

You deserve the best.

"What I didn't deserve
was worst,
But what I deserve now
is the Best."

"The special thing about trains is that they teach us the importance of punctuality in every situation, no matter we're being late or being for the late."

"You know what The Best Part about me is that I have you. You'll never know this fact but I always knew from the start that I have to keep you forever and this is

the only reason I wanted to capture every moment of us so that one day we could look back at the reel of moments in our beautiful life spent together played over and over again like our most Favourite Romantic Movie."

"You were never out of time to start something off new."

"There's much more important things in life than to just earn money because, It doesn't matter how much money you make, But whom you spend it with."

LIFE

"I wish I could wake up with amnesia and forget about the regrets I'm living with because the people will never let me do it and my life is too short to regret anything."

"Life is not about the right path with right decision but a path with a decision making it righteous to your own self-explained terms satisfying else terms if may."

"Life is a mixture of shades. Sometimes dark is horror and sometimes dark is fantasy."

"Money won't assure you life but longevity if possible."

"This world is a bird cage to me but what kept me from ending up as a slave was the flight I have longed for."

"Inside every Self-Made man, there is a 'pain' of not having what you want but a 'courage' chasing those dreams off until they make you one."

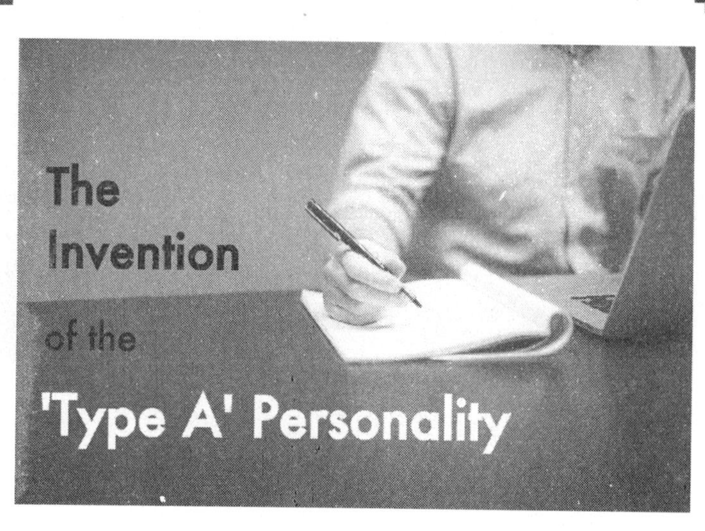

"You don't need Super Powers to be a Hero. But an extraordinary Self-Made Personality to be one'."

"Life can be full of selfish people but finding the selflessness in yourself to see in others is a big task. If you succeeded in it, you've got a friend but if you didn't, then your time for the task has got wasted."

"Life is stepping into the dark to get the righteous horizon of truth."

"Embrace the trials and tribulations and that is what builds you and strengthens you."

"Life is all about choices and thereafter consequences. We can't choose the cards that are dealt to us but what we can choose is how to play and manipulate the game."

"Life—

The one in need is the sufferer of greed indeed."

"To me psychology is irrational certification to term psychos as rational."

"Life taught me enough to establish myself as Mr. Me today besides knowing all of my internal instincts and making my bad habits extinct."

"I've seen ourselves blaming our own luck and destiny for the faults in our lives. What if I say those were actually 'The Fault In Our Starts' because blaming destiny, luck and people won't make a difference but hardworking, faith and patience will always do."

"Don't keep searching for the truth, just let go off the lies you'd been confined to."

"I hide an ocean of emotions with notions and various motions defining my life-perceptive proportions."

"An act of providence can prevent a physical death but won't prevent someone from having a real death on their guilty conscience."

"If there are specific days of gods then there might be specific days of your visits to the holy places and your favoured requests approvals."

"Fear nothing but
Conscience
Believe nothing but
Science
But when both fails
Hope nothing but God."

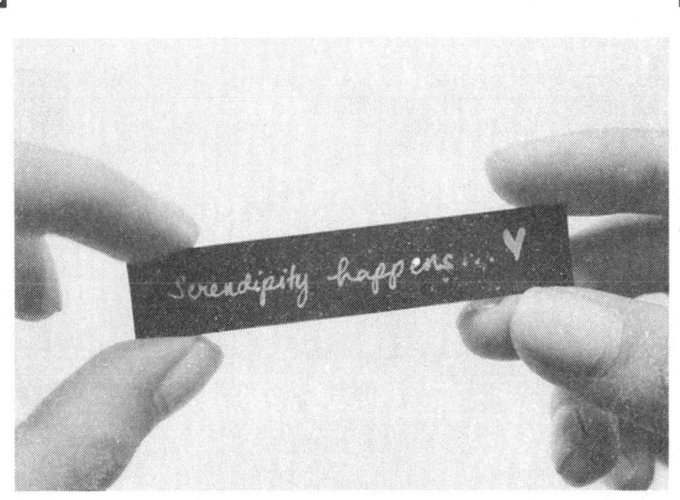

"I always have searched for best in the world, then this serendipity happens."

"Money can make you look younger but not young again."

"Chances are temporary and regrets are permanent."

NATURE

"Mother nature is the perfect escape for my life problems, frustrations and depression. It nurtures my mind, body and soul with great positivity like my own biological mother."

FOR PUNJAB

"The Beauty of this City beholds me in a Heavenly feel I always seek for."

"Each droplet of this
every 'RAIN' realises me
of my pain.
My pain realises me of
mine lifelong memories
and mine love being
insane
How strange is this Rain!
With some, it shares
happiness
And, with some, it
shares pain."

"Mother nature loves everyone perennially irrespective of one's wealth and status."

"I could've never known in whole of my childhood that why Green has been my all-time favourite colour since I got to realise that how much mesmerised I'm with the beauty of the Mother Nature."

"Nature is the only stress buster I've known and also it turns out to be the best every time."

"Nature is the best anti-depressant therapy and also cheaper than medication."

"The one thing I can always have time for in my busy life is a walk with my Mother Nature."

"The similarity between both the Mother Nature and my biological mother is that they both have sacrificed their resources to raise me as a better man."

"Nature reminds me to stop, to look around and to believe in something else because there is always something more than I always seek for."

"Nature could heal what was broken and patience could heal what is unspoken."

FITNESS

"The '3G MANTRA' to complete a marathon:

1. Get up

2. Gear up

3. Give yourself up to the field."

"Healthy attitude is a wealthy gratitude to your own life."

"The biggest achievement
is Health
The biggest wealth is
Wisdom
The biggest feeling is Love
The biggest weapon is
Patience
The biggest tonic is
Laughter
And surprisingly they
all are Free!"

"Look like a champion and run like a pro"

"It's a lively self-
comparison
It's time to be a Paragon
Worthy being an Amazon
Health for life is
the message of a
MARATHON"

"A diseased person can still run for his health But an infected person can never"

(Infected here is quoted to infection of greedy and money-minded)

"Completing a Marathon is a self-created milestone of life."

*"Health is optimism
Wealth is materialism
And choosing the right
path to attain them is
spiritualism."*

"Ageing is just a belief to regret your existence for non-accomplishments, irrespective of those who died spiritualistically with self-accomplishments."

FASHION

"To me, Clothing is a form of Self-Expression to say Who you are in What you wear and to Reflect the real 'You' in the World."

For Hardworking Designer

"You know what's special about this suit is You coz to people it reflects my class and my style but to us it reflects my idea and your hard work."

"My Colours of Style may include Dark, Basic or the Same but glamour of my SWAG, it's Fascinating, Progressive, Impressive but Never the Same."

"My Poses, My Pictures,
My Way
Live My Life In My Own
Way
Coz I know better How to
make My Day."

"To me fashion is a conscience of playing with different colours so as to make oneself beautiful from outside and comfortable from inside."

"Wearing suit is a main determinant to my own significance."

"I would put on my favourite suit and tie when I'll go to my own first book launch event, Coz that's what suits are for; they make me feel special when I need to."

SUCCESS

"May be all those sleepless nights of solitude were worth giving me a reason to self-explore about the meaning of different colours of life which made me an author of a book which you are reading today."

"Worthlessness of possessions sometimes might frustrate but earning a big sum could buy some 'Peace' at 5 Star properties."

"To the ones who didn't believe my Worth Today They are Talking at my back because of my Possessions."

"I am thankful to those people who didn't believe in me

Because of them I started believing in myself, so far the best strength I know."

"A failure can unleash a Storm of Success."

"We are what we are!
If it does change, then we
aren't what we weren't.
To be is to be and to not,
again is to be of what
is not meant to be but
happens to be."

"Control of the quantity, quality and money according to the code of business discipline – these form the basis of an ideal deal here for the wise businessman."

"To be somewhere far, you have to let go off your opinions why not to go coz after all, time is just a standardised set of numbers to be achieved."

"I am original.
My uniqueness is my authenticity."

"Don't try to be better than anyone else but YOU."

"I definitely have to be successful because I've a very expensive taste."

"Sometimes shoe contact speaks more than eye contact."

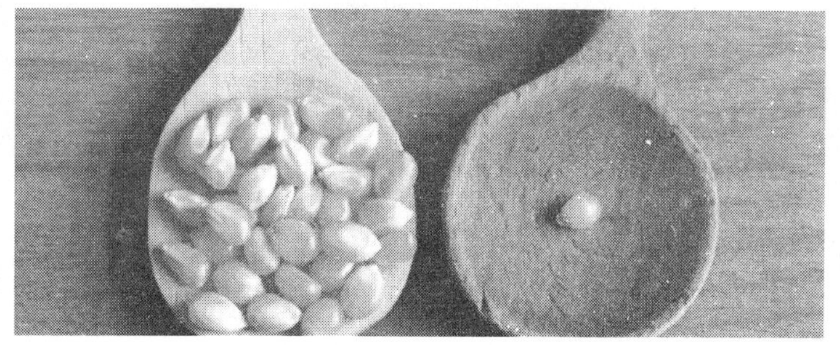

"More is never enough and less is always less."

"How could have you explored about yourself if you haven't taken your chances and did the mistakes yet. May be you are too much afraid to fall down or too much worried for what happens if you may fly."

"Vulnerability to susceptibility eliminates the weaknesses we're confined to in order to achieve our goal."

Dr. Tanbir Dhingra

When he did his first stage singing performance at the age of 6, *Tanbir Dhingra* could not imagine that this song '*Papa Kehte Hain Bada Naam Karega*' meaning their son will make them proud one day; would take him from his family in Punjab to Uttar Pradesh, on the other side of Indian globe.

Today, he is a ***Bachelor of Medicine & Surgery***. He was born in 1993 to a *Sikh Family* on the festive land of martyrs and freedom fighters, *Punjab*.

By the age of 12 from his experience in first love, *Tanbir* discovered his true vocation in literature: to be a writer. He's a poet who draws, an actor who sings, a dancer who designs; a full time blogger, innovative like his fashion blog, social networking addict, works to travel around. His writing record testifies to certain dexterity in languages like English, Hindi, and Punjabi. Above all he loves his coffee.

Contact:
dhingratanbir@gmail.com
www.drtanbirdhingra.com
www.facebook.com/MyFeelingsMyPoetryFromMyHeart/
http://thebrokeninfinity.wordpress.com/